limestone, the tower was adorned with elaborate marble carvings and may have stood in the center of a vast courtyard surrounded by lush gardens.

The light of the Pharos was most likely produced by fires tended ceaselessly by slaves, who also performed the arduous task of carting the wood to the tower's summit. The lantern may also have held giant reflectors to increase the light's visibility, which reached a distance of 42 miles (67.57 km). At times, particularly during the day, the voluminous smoke that expelled forth from the Pharos served as an even better guide than the fire.

The Pharos lit the skies for more than ten centuries, impressing the likes of Julius Caesar and Pliny the Elder, and the mighty tower endured unlighted for another five hundred years. Its service endured many serious disruptions, including the seventh-century destruction of its lantern during the Arab conquest of Egypt. Several earthquakes wrought damage over the years, and finally an earthquake in the fourteenth century brought the structure to ruins. Yet even in its final years it had remained awe-inspiring; not long before its destruction a visitor declared that "the whole is imperishable, although the waves of the sea continually break against its northern face."

Renowned for their skill and pride in building roads, bridges, walls, aqueducts, and many other structures, the Romans left strangely few records of their lighthouses. Tradition holds that they erected at least thirty lighthouses, the best known and largest of which was a four-story tower built about 50 A.D.; it stood at Ostia, the port of Rome, at the mouth of the River Tiber. Ravenna, on the Adriatic Sea in northern Italy, also received a lighthouse, probably as early as the first century; by the fourth century this city had become a major center of

OPPOSITE
To facilitate expanding trade activity, maritime countries throughout Europe began to increase the number of lighthouses along their coasts. An eighteenth-century painting by Cioci Antonio depicts the lighthouse and port at Villa La Tana, Italy.

Lighthouse designs the world over share common general plans. This cross-sectional view shows the plan of a German lighthouse.

trade and certainly a logical place for a lighthouse, with a harbor capable of accommodating well over two hundred ships. Another of the Seven Wonders, the Colossus of Rhodes, was said to have served as an aid to navigators, with lights maintained in the statue's eyes or raised hand, but there is little evidence that the immense figure ever really served as a lighthouse.

The Romans also placed lighthouses in their provinces, including one on each side of the English Channel. The towers they built on the cliffs of Boulogne in France and the cliffs of Dover in England were most likely the first ones installed in Western Europe after its conquest by Rome. Choosing these elevated sites made the towers less costly; with only 80 feet (24.4 m) of construction they achieved lights that soared almost 400 feet (122 m) above the sea.

MEDIEVAL LIGHTHOUSES

Early lights were generally built close to shore in more accessible areas, to which supplies could be brought easily. But rocks and reefs many miles offshore also presented great danger to ships. One of the earliest and most courageous offshore efforts to erect a lighthouse occurred 5 miles (8.04 km) off the coast of France on the small island of Cordouan. According to legend, the first navigational aid on the island came at the behest of Charlemagne himself, who had a chapel built on the island and ordered the sounding of trumpets to warn passing vessels. Erected in the ninth century as an aid to ships in the Bordeaux wine trade, the first lighthouse on the site was supposedly built by Charlemagne's son

A Light by Any Other Name

The only one of the Seven Wonders with daily practical application, the Pharos served for so long and became so famous that some version of this word means lighthouse in many different languages. Pharus, the Latin term, gave rise to the French phare and the Italian faro. The study of lighthouses is known in English as pharology, another word that owes its derivation to this ancient structure.

The Skerryvore Lighthouse, off the coast of Scotland, was built to withstand the punishing currents of the North Sea.

SKERRYVORE LIGHTHOUSE, ON THE COAST OF SCOTLAND. 1854

Louis the Pious. Supported by funds collected from the area's ships, the Cordouan light was tended by monks, a common practice throughout the medieval period.

A new lighthouse erected on Cordouan in the late fourteenth century included a chapel and living quarters for the monks. By the late sixteenth century this lighthouse had become irreparable and an elaborate replacement was constructed. Intended to take two years, this extremely difficult undertaking wound up taking more than twenty. Simply ferrying the workers to and from this distant site required six boats. Once building began it was discovered that the island was beginning to disappear, so a sturdy wall and parapet were constructed in an attempt to stave off the encroaching sea. Eventually a magnificent structure resulted, complete with statues, pillars, a royal chapel, and a room for the king. In an unusual variation, the spiral staircase was located off to the side to prevent the main portion of the structure from becoming soiled by workers bringing wood and equipment up to the lantern. The ornate tower attained the height of a sixteen-story building, only to lose 25 feet (7.62 m) off the top when it was struck by lightning in 1612. Yet it continued to serve for hundreds of years and helped to convince naysayers that it was indeed possible to construct a workable lighthouse in the middle of the sea.

As trading activity increased during the Middle Ages, England, Ireland, France, Germany, Turkey, and Italy recognized the need for more lighthouses to illuminate their coasts and facilitate their additional shipping capabilities. One of the most famous Italian lighthouses is the one at Genoa, where Antonio Colombo, uncle of Christopher Columbus, served as keeper in 1449. First built in the twelfth century, the original lighthouse was

Now inactive, **Price Creek Lighthouse** was erected to guide vessels through the mouth of the Cape Fear River, part of a dangerous expanse of waters along the southern coast of North Carolina. *Southport, North Carolina*

CHAPTER TWO

Building the Towers

As the sun peeks through the storm-darkened sky, a few sailors row small ferries from an anchored ship to the wave-beaten lighthouse in this undated engraving.

OPPOSITE
A noted landmark in the Chincoteague National Wildlife Refuge, Assateague Lighthouse stands 142 feet tall, with the focal plane of its light at 154 feet above sea level. *Chincoteague, Virginia*

More than a thousand years ago, Viking sea charts labeled the Cape Cod region *Straumey*, meaning "an island possessed of strong currents." But most early European voyagers lacked even primitive maps of these new lands, and for centuries the uncharted shores of North America presented unknown hazards to sailors brave enough to explore the coast. With no lights visible to brighten night skies at sea, the only navigational aids available were crude shipboard tools, seafaring experience, and maritime instinct. As more and more ships reached the New World, inhabitants began lighting signal fires along the coast to guide their way. In 1673, on the bleak headland of Point Allerton near Boston, was lit the first primitive approximation of a lighthouse in the Americas. Though hardly more than a light on a pole, it was a beginning.

EARLY LIGHTS IN THE NEW WORLD

The history of American lighthouses officially begins in 1716. At the request of the area's merchants, the Province of Massachusetts that

The harbour lies below me, with, on the far side, one long granite wall stretching out into the sea, with a curve outwards at the end of it, in the middle of which is a lighthouse.

—*Bram Stoker,* Dracula

quently to keep the lamp from smoking. The late 1700s saw the introduction of oil-burning spider lamps, which were suspended by iron chains from the top of the lantern. Though they emitted better light, keepers found their caustic fumes intolerable.

A major innovation occurred in 1781 when Swiss physicist Aimé Argand developed a lamp that utilized a hollow wick, allowing more air to flow around the flame. The additional oxygen made for a much brighter flame. Around 1812, the power of the Argand lamp was increased with the addition of parabolic reflectors and a magnifier.

Though the skeletal ironwork of Rawley Point Lighthouse looks surprisingly modern, it was erected in 1894 to replace a brick tower built twenty years earlier, contemporaneous with the dwelling. *Two Rivers, Wisconsin*

OPPOSITE
Renowned for its twin light towers, the community of Cape Elizabeth was outraged in 1924 when the Bureau of Lighthouses declared an end to multiple-tower stations. Though only the eastern tower still stands, the station is still commonly known as Two Lights. Edward Hopper's The Lighthouse at Two Lights was painted five years after the western tower was dismantled. *Cape Elizabeth, Maine*

PREVIOUS PAGE
Most lighthouses are equipped with a number of other buildings, such as a boathouse and keeper's quarters. The clean design of the1876 cylindrical iron, brick-lined tower of Nobska Point Lighthouse compliments the stark lines of the buildings beside it. *Falmouth, Massachusetts*

The World's Largest Lens

The Stevensons were an extraordinary family of Scottish lighthouse engineers who dominated their country's lighthouse service throughout the nineteenth century and well into this one. (Novelist Robert Louis Stevenson, who began his career as a lighthouse engineer, was a fourth-generation member of the Stevenson lighthouse clan.) They developed a type of lens called the hyperradiant lens, whose focal distance—measured from the light to the inside of the lens—makes it the largest lens ever produced. The hyperradiant lens has a focal distance of over 52 inches (132 cm), compared to 36 inches (91.4 cm) for a first-order Fresnel. Only about twelve lenses of this type were in use throughout the world in the early twentieth century.

The only hyperradiant lens ever acquired by the United States was installed in 1909 at Makapuu Lighthouse. Located on the island of Oahu, this site was deemed in need of a lighthouse in 1905, when the Lighthouse Board declared, "All deep-sea commerce between Honolulu and Puget Sound, the Pacific coast of the United States, Mexico and Central America, including Panama, passes Makapuu Head, and . . . there is not a single light on the whole northern coast of the Hawaiian Islands to guide ships or warn them of their approach to land, after a voyage of several thousand miles." Now automated, the still-active light at Makapuu boasts an immense lens with an inside diameter of 8.5 feet (2.59 m).

Aye on the shores of darkness there is light,

And precipices show untrodden green,

There is a budding morrow in midnight,

There is a triple sight in blindness keen.

—John Keats

OPPOSITE
**Stone structures have proven
to be the most durable
kind of lighthouse. After a gale
destroyed the first, wooden
lighthouse in 1816, a stone
replacement was built at the
entrance to Narragansett
Bay. The current granite tower
of Point Judith Lighthouse
was erected in 1856.**
Narragansett, Rhode Island

**Deemed by the Lighthouse
Board a "very important light,"
Montauk Lighthouse was
ranked tenth of the nation's
thirty-eight light stations
that required first-order lens.**
Long Island, New York

The true breakthrough in lighthouse illumination came about 1815 when an engineer named Augustin-Jean Fresnel invented the most efficient lighthouse lens of all. Resembling a beehive, the Fresnel lens consisted of a configuration of glass belts to magnify and refract light. By 1859, Fresnel lenses had replaced reflectors in most United States lighthouses. Sperm oil was still the most common illuminant, but because it was costly, lard oil became standard in the 1860s and was widely used until 1877, when kerosene gained prominence. Although electricity was introduced in the early twentieth century, it did not become universally employed for several decades. Many of today's electric lighthouses still employ the Fresnel lens.

**Built in 1827, Pemaquid
Point Lighthouse received
its fourth-order Fresnel
lens in the 1850s. The
light was automated in
1934.** *Pemaquid Point,
Maine*

the light and perform other essential tasks. Often the keeper's wife officially served as assistant keeper.

The family of the keeper was called on to assist with as many duties as possible. When the daily chores were complete, it was time to turn to general maintenance tasks such as minor equipment repairs, patching cracks in the tower walls, or replacing damaged panes of glass in the lantern. At least once a year the corroded metal of the lantern required refurbishing. If the tower was whitewashed, as many were, it called for the arduous task of repainting, which entailed sitting in a basket far above the ground and hoisting oneself up and down by means of a pulley system. (Women were exempt from participating in this painting task.) The seemingly endless staircase spiraling up into the tower also needed new paint once a year, conducted in a such a way as to keep the stairs usable at all times to reach the lantern. And there was the constant task of polishing the brass, which was quickly dulled by fog and salt water. In addition to the exertions required to make the tower run smoothly, the entire light station needed continual diligence for everything from common housekeeping to detailed recordkeeping.

Though there was little time for idleness with so many chores to complete, lighthouse dwellers did find themselves with occasional time on their hands. In their isolated setting, with no readymade activities to hand nor a community to participate in, keepers and their families had to develop their own recreation. To break the monotony they often took up hobbies such as boat building, wood carving, basket weaving, rug hooking, tailoring, painting, or music. Others devoted

The first light station in British Columbia was the charmingly designed Fisgard Lighthouse, tended by keepers until 1928. *Victoria, British Columbia*

OPPOSITE
One of the West Coast's first eight lights, the old Point Loma Lighthouse was so high—462 feet above the sea—that low clouds often obscured it. Replaced by a newer station in 1891, the original 1855 Cape Cod–style structure now houses an exhibit detailing the life of a keeper's family. *San Diego, California*

Clean lanterns, lenses, and windows are imperative in lighthouses, and maintaining the mechanism was in itself a full-time job. *Winchester Bay, Oregon*

OPPOSITE
Situated to the west of the entrance to Muscongus Bay, Pemaquid Point Lighthouse sits atop spectacular bluffs that make the station a popular tourist destination. *Pemaquid Point, Maine*

PREVIOUS PAGE
Encased in steel plates painted eye-popping red, Holland Harbor South Pierhead Lighthouse features a twin-gabled roof indicative of the heavy Dutch influence in the region. *Holland, Michigan*

themselves to the study of sea birds, seashells, or local artifacts. Also popular were fishing and hunting, which not only provided a diversion but yielded a ready supply of food as well. A monthly excursion to the mainland to buy food and collect mail also offered a much-needed opportunity to do a bit of socializing and to keep up with developments in the outside world.

Growing up in the unique atmosphere of a light station, many sons and daughters of lighthouse keepers knew little of the outside world. Education presented many problems, and keepers' families arrived at various solutions. The nearest schools were generally too far for a daily commute, nor would the prospect of traveling over a rough sea make it any easier. Although many keepers received additional finances for educating their children, wages were usually too low to afford room and board, even though the school itself might be free. And the children themselves, accustomed as they were to a

In 1876, the Lighthouse Board created circulating libraries offering a wide choice of reading materials to the keepers' family, who anticipated with great delight the arrival of new books every three months. The board ordered the libraries make the rounds of "isolated light-houses of the higher orders, where there are keepers with families, who will read and appreciate the books the Libraries contain." By 1885, over four hundred libraries were in circulation. Each library contained about forty publications, including novels, biographies, religious subjects, and magazines. Many of the books were acquired through donations from people who wanted to help provide diversions for lonely keepers.

The brick tower and dwelling of Point aux Barques Lighthouse—captured here in watercolor by Robert Wilson Fagan—date from an 1857 rebuilding of the station. The second dwelling was added in 1908. *Port Austin, Michigan*

LADIES OF THE LAMP

The position of lighthouse keeper, though typically considered to belong to men, employed a great number of women as well, who were often the wives of keepers and served as assistant keepers. The fifth auditor of the treasury—responsible for lighthouse administration until the advent of the Lighthouse Board—gave particular preference to women from 1820 to 1852, specifying that a recently widowed wife of a keeper should be tendered the job before anyone else. So many women accepted this offer that by 1852 the United States boasted thirty female keepers. Even after the board began discouraging the hiring of women in 1852, many women managed to obtain the job.

After the death of her husband, Kate Walker was appointed to his job as keeper of Staten Island's Robbins Reef Lighthouse, retiring at the age of seventy-three. For years she ferried her two children to school each day, rowing over a mile each way. During her lengthy tenure (from 1896 to 1919), she saved fifty lives by her own estimate. All this at a station that could only be entered by reaching out from her boat, grabbing a shaky ladder, and climbing up into the kitchen.

OPPOSITE

The keeper's quarters and lighthouse at Wind Point combines a 108-foot Italianate brick tower with a traditional Mid-Western style farmhouse on southwestern shore of Lake Michigan. *Racine, Wisconsin*

Perched precariously outside
the lantern, keepers scrub
the glass clean to maintain
maximum brightness from
the station's light.

Matinicus Rock Lighthouse, an extremely isolated station on the rugged midcoast of Maine, was home to Abbie Burgess, one of the most dedicated women to serve as lighthouse keeper. The daughter of Matinicus Rock's keeper, Abbie first demonstrated her dedication as a teenager in the 1850s when her father became stranded on the mainland and she took charge of the station during an incredible four-week storm that sent waves crashing over their roof, completely flooding the keeper's quarters and forcing them to take shelter in the tower. In addition to caring for their invalid mother and coping with the furious storm, she and her three younger sisters succeeded in running the light each and every night. A year later she again performed her duties heroically in her father's absence; this time the storm lasted three weeks and the family nearly ran out of food, but the light never failed. In 1861, she married the son of the station's new keeper; together they ran Matinicus Rock for fourteen years, later transferring to

OPPOSITE
Built in 1871, Yaquina Bay
Lighthouse had served for
only three years when the
Lighthouse Board declared it
unnecessary, since the
Yaquina Head Lighthouse
stood just a few miles away.
Local residents saved the
landmark from planned de-
struction in 1946; it is now a
museum. *Newport, Oregon*

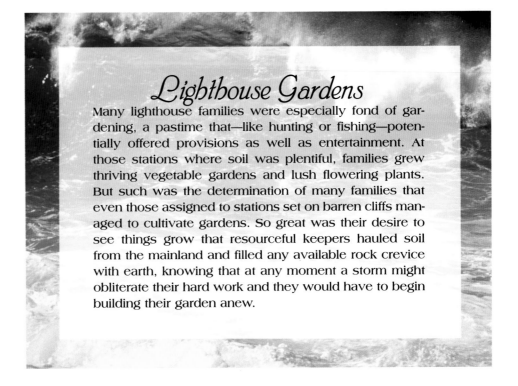

Lighthouse Gardens

Many lighthouse families were especially fond of gardening, a pastime that—like hunting or fishing—potentially offered provisions as well as entertainment. At those stations where soil was plentiful, families grew thriving vegetable gardens and lush flowering plants. But such was the determination of many families that even those assigned to stations set on barren cliffs managed to cultivate gardens. So great was their desire to see things grow that resourceful keepers hauled soil from the mainland and filled any available rock crevice with earth, knowing that at any moment a storm might obliterate their hard work and they would have to begin building their garden anew.

The epitome of the quaint New England lighthouse, Stage Harbor Light is captured on a snowy winter's day in this watercolor by James Strickland.

OPPOSITE
The compact tower, dwelling, and outbuildings of Prospect Harbor Point Lighthouse sit close to the shore on the rocky Maine coast. *Prospect Harbor, Maine*

Whitehead Light Station, where Abbie remained assistant keeper until 1889.

One of the most renowned keepers of all time was a woman named Ida Lewis. Born in Newport, Rhode Island in 1842, she performed her first rescue at age 15; her last at age 65. When her father, the first keeper of Newport Harbor's Lime Rock Lighthouse, was paralyzed by a stroke soon after his appointment, she assumed his duties. She saved many people, but her most famous and daring rescue occurred during a blizzard in 1869, when she saved three men whose boat had overturned in the raging storm. After *Harper's Weekly* placed her on their cover that year to acknowledge her bravery, people learned of her earlier heroism. Though she regretted her lost privacy, fame brought with it long-overdue recognition of her years of hard work. The governor of Rhode Island learned that she received neither pay nor title for doing a lighthouse keeper's job and his efforts ensured that she was officially appointed to the post. As her fame spread she received many awards, as well as visits from President Ulysses S. Grant and a number of other important officials. When she died in 1911, the Bureau of Lighthouses changed the station's name to the Ida Lewis Rock Lighthouse, one of the very few lights to be named after a person and the only keeper to be so honored.

The last woman lighthouse keeper in the United States was Fannie Salter, who retired from her position after twenty-two years of service at Maryland's Turkey Point Lighthouse on Chesapeake Bay. After her retirement in 1947, the light was given over to automation.

THE RAVAGES OF NATURE

As solitary as their lives often were, many keepers must have longed for an even quieter life when faced with the extremes of weather they continually faced. The exposed location of the lighthouse placed it well in the way of many meteorological excesses. Wild winds and torrential rains churned the seas, producing waves of dizzying heights, often tall enough to sweep over the lantern. Lightning damaged many a tower until lightning rods were eventually installed. Hurricanes have toppled a number of lights, including the first Key West lighthouse, Rhode Island's Prudence Island light, and Palmer Island light in New Bedford, Massachusetts. In 1938, a terrible hurricane ravaged many New England lighthouses. Winter storms were also particularly taxing: Blizzards and ice buildup obscured visibility, interfered with station functions, and sometimes trapped keepers inside or prevented them from entering; and bone-chilling cold made even the simplest tasks arduous.

Minot's Ledge Light is considered by many to be the nation's most dangerous lighthouse. Located near Cohasset, just south of Boston, the treacherously rocky and wave-swept offshore region witnessed many shipwrecks before an iron-pile light was begun in 1847. When the station went into service in 1850, the keeper expressed doubts about the structure's durability. His successor also came to doubt its ability to withstand the extremes of the site's conditions. After a terrible gale in April 1851, the local paper declared, "Great apprehensions are

A Unique Winter Hazard

Coastal lighthouses experience a wide range of treacherous conditions, but the salt of the oceans at least prevents a substantial amount of ice from building up. The stations along the Great Lakes are not so lucky. The combination of high winds, subzero temperatures, and frequent blizzards acting upon sites surrounded by fresh water can lead to terrifying results. Surrounded by towering snowdrifts, entire towers have become encased in ice, impairing their function and imprisoning their keepers inside or preventing them from gaining access. Lake Huron's Spectacle Reef Lighthouse—built after two wrecks occurred on a dangerous reef in 1868—took several years to construct. When keepers arrived to open it for the first time in the spring of 1874, ice had piled more than 30 feet (9.15 m) up the tower; they had to chop it away to reach the door.

OPPOSITE
Heavy clouds roll in toward Heceta Head Lighthouse, which guards the central Oregon coast north of the Siuslaw River.
Florence, Oregon

The rocky, trecherous coasts
of New England were the
sights of many shipwrecks,
and were a breeding ground
for "mooncussers"—pirates
who awaited (and perhaps
even helped cause) ship-
wrecks in hopes of looting
the valuable cargo.

FOLLOWING PAGE
A storm approaches West
Breakwater Lighthouse, just
northeast of Cleveland
on the shore of Lake Erie.
Fairport, Ohio

the ocean. Keepers and supplies had to be hoisted up by derrick 75 feet (almost 23 m) onto a concrete landing. After a relentless eighteen months of construction the lantern was lit in 1881, unfortunately four weeks too late to save the twenty men who perished just a mile from Tillamook in a wreck precipitated by a heavy fog. Though the light has since been decommissioned, it served for nearly eighty years under the care of five keepers at all times because of the extreme danger of the site. One keeper even reported green water streaming over the very top of the tower on one occasion; on another he witnessed a storm that created waves strong enough to tear rocks from the island and hurl them through the metal dome of the lantern. Several years later a winter storm propelled stones, seaweed, and fish into the lantern and smashed the lens. Hundred-foot waves regularly pounded the station, whose perilous situation earned it the nickname "the hoodoo light."

DARING RESCUES

Throughout the history of lighthouses, keepers and their assistants have performed many acts of bravery. Nearly every one of them took

This nineteenth-century watercolor depicts a heroic rescue performed an English lighthouse keeper and his daughter. James and Grace Darling rowed their small boat through the heavy seas of a terrible storm to save the passengers and crew of a wrecked ship in 1838.

At the mercy of the raging sea, a British warship is battered as easily as a tiny row-boat. *A First-Rate Man-of-War Driving on a Reef of Rocks, Foundering in a Gale*, a nineteenth-century oil by George Philip Reinagle, captures the sense of raw power unleashed by a fearsome storm.

The fogbound Yaquina Head Lighthouse appears to hover mysteriously between land and sky, the dangerously craggy coast all but obscured in the mist-shrouded air. *Newport, Oregon*

their perches in the rigging, had virtually given up hope. After the keeper's unsuccessful attempts to throw a line aboard, a towering wave dashed the vessel against the rocks. Finally Hanna—eventually aided by neighbors who came to help with the rescue—managed to haul the nearly paralyzed mariners to shore and carry them through the deep snow to the fog signal station. Though the captain had been lost, the two men did survive, thanks to the dedication of Keeper Hanna.

THE CURSE OF THE WRECKERS

Saving the lives of sailors and passengers was actually a secondary consideration in the decision to build a lighthouse. The immediate purpose was to enable safe passage of the ship's cargo, the value of which was often deemed far greater than that of the people on board. In the eyes of the merchants and ship owners, the cost of building a

OPPOSITE
The 51-foot-tall Grand Haven South Pierhead Inner Light guards Lake Michigan's eastern shore on a bleak winter's day as ice encroaches on the catwalk. *Ottawa County, Michigan*

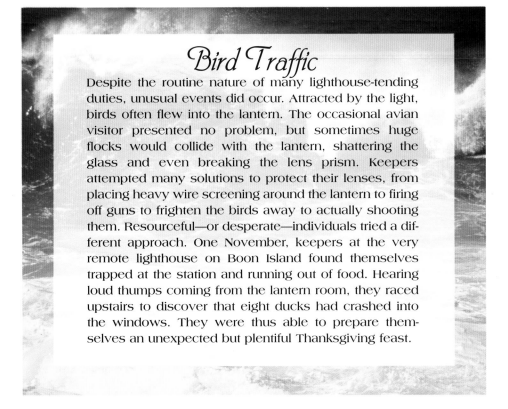

Bird Traffic

Despite the routine nature of many lighthouse-tending duties, unusual events did occur. Attracted by the light, birds often flew into the lantern. The occasional avian visitor presented no problem, but sometimes huge flocks would collide with the lantern, shattering the glass and even breaking the lens prism. Keepers attempted many solutions to protect their lenses, from placing heavy wire screening around the lantern to firing off guns to frighten the birds away to actually shooting them. Resourceful—or desperate—individuals tried a different approach. One November, keepers at the very remote lighthouse on Boon Island found themselves trapped at the station and running out of food. Hearing loud thumps coming from the lantern room, they raced upstairs to discover that eight ducks had crashed into the windows. They were thus able to prepare themselves an unexpected but plentiful Thanksgiving feast.

Perched on a cliff high
above the shore, the
Heceta Head Lighthouse
ensures a safer passage
to vessels navigating the
rocky Oregon coast.
Florence, Oregon

CHAPTER FIVE

Lighting the Future

Erected in 1792, the first Cape Henry Lighthouse exhibited large cracks by 1870, when the Lighthouse Board declared it "in danger of being thrown down by some heavy gale." In 1881 this distinctively patterned tower was built beside the first, but the original remains standing to this day. *Virginia Beach, Virginia*

The arrival of automation came at the turn of the century. The first lighthouse powered by electricity was northern New Jersey's Navesink Light, where an electric arc bivalve lens was installed in 1898. The Lighthouse Board began testing electricity for general lighthouse use around 1900, but the majority of United States lighthouses were not converted to electricity until the 1920s and 1930s because they were located at great distance from power lines. The introduction of electricity gradually resulted in the automation of virtually all lighthouses, eliminating the need for resident keepers.

Quite a few modern lighthouses are vastly different structures from the traditional lighthouse. With today's technology, what was once an elaborate station complete with tower, dwellings, and workshops has been reduced to a simple platform or post that provides everything necessary to operate the streamlined lenses and self-contained lights now in use, lights that turn themselves on right before sunset and wink

The Lighthouse was then a silvery, misty-looking tower with a yellow eye, that opened suddenly, and softly in the evening.

Virginia Woolf, To the Lighthouse

off just after the sun rises. Technological advances have drastically reduced the size of lights and lenses and made them weatherproof. Coupled with other mechanization, such as radio beacons and radar, such smaller, lighter apparatus needs only a basic setup for efficient operation. Where once a whole family might be needed to keep a station running smoothly, nowadays a lighthouse generally requires human attention only about four times a year. Contemporary keepers—all members of the Coast Guard—are known as ANTs, short for Aid to Navigation Teams.

Although Fresnel lenses are still used in a number of lighthouses, Coast Guard personnel have installed a new system of automation known as ATON, which employs plastic lenses styled after the Fresnel design. The lenses contain six or more small bulbs on a belt; when a bulb burns out, the belt moves another one into place. In many locations, solar panels have been installed to recharge the lights' batteries.

Fewer than sixty stations retained their keepers by the late 1960s; today, keepers are virtually a relic of the past. The United States Coast Guard—the current administrator of the country's lighthouses—set out in 1989 to complete its plan to automate all lights under its command. Although the Coast Guard did not initiate automation (it was begun by the Bureau of Lighthouses), it has done the most in instituting this economical process. The only fully staffed lighthouse still in operation is the one at Boston Harbor. Originally scheduled for

Going Electric

Surprisingly, the very first use of electricity in a lighthouse capacity did not occur in a lighthouse. When an electric arc was installed in the Statue of Liberty in 1886, it became the first electrified structure to serve as a lighthouse. Now a national monument, the statue is no longer considered a navigational aid, but for a brief time the lady and her torch did help to guide ships into New York Harbor.

Destroyed by a storm in 1984,
Great Point Lighthouse was
replicated in 1987, complete
with a solar-powered cofferdam
to protect it from future erosion.
Nantucket, Massachusetts

Perched on a bluff severely threatened by erosion, Southeast Lighthouse is endangered by the encroaching sea. Plans are underway to move the station to a safer spot. *Block Island, Rhode Island*

LIGHTHOUSE CULTURE

Emblematic of selfless dedication and poetic isolation, lighthouses are a popular motif in today's culture. Countless collectible items feature lighthouse themes, and seven states have placed lighthouses on their license plates. Organizations as diverse as a major insurance company and the eponymous association for the blind have chosen the lighthouse as a corporate logo, based its symbolic power as a beacon to illuminate the darkness. Literature has turned to the lighthouse as an extension of the concept of the ivory tower: a symbol of the timeless yearning to retreat from life's daily urgency, to abide in a tranquil setting removed from everyday cares. No matter that the reality of the keeper's existence was often far from peaceful and comprised an endless round of daily tasks; the modern imagination has idealized lighthouse living and proclaimed it sublime.

Technology has drastically changed the age-old traditions under which lighthouses operated, but it has certainly not diminished the charm these structures continue to exude, nor the fervor invested by many in efforts to preserve and maintain them, nor the power they continue to hold over the imagination. And technology has had another sort of ramification on lighthouse lore, one that no engineer, administrator, or keeper of the traditional tower could have anticipated in the heyday of the lighthouse: the impact of the Internet. There are now literally thousands of electronic sites devoted to lighthouses, covering everything from serious historical, architectural studies (complete with full-color pictures) to urgent preservation efforts; from geographical surveys of the world's lights to individuals' personal preferences about the greatest towers; from book stores and gift shops hawking lighthouse-related items to hobbyists who create lighthouse-themed crafts.

So You Want to Be a Lighthouse Keeper

According to a list originally compiled by the United States Lighthouse Society in San Francisco, there are nineteen lighthouses around the country offering guest accommodations. Most of these range from bed-and-breakfast establishments resembling country inns to simple youth hostel setups. But the New Dungeness Light Station in Sequim, Washington, gives visitors first-hand experience at tending a lighthouse. Established in 1857 and overhauled in 1927, the station stands on a remote sandspit in the Straits of Juan de Fuca. The light is staffed entirely by volunteers, twenty-four hours a day, year round. Each Friday or Saturday, a new team of two couples arrives (sometimes with children), to spend the week living at the furnished keeper's quarters (built in 1904). For their week's tour of duty they are assigned specific tasks to maintain the house and grounds, and, of course, to keep the light burning.

Yaquina Head Lighthouse was originally known as Cape Foulweather Light because the building materials were inadvertantly landed at this spot in 1873, rather than at their intended destination of Cape Foulweather, four miles to the north. *Newport, Oregon*

The slender hexagonal tower of San Felipe Lighthouse soars above the landscape.
Baja, California

Despite the relentless commercialism evident in much of today's lighthouse paraphernalia, the very fact that the lighthouse still enjoys such vast popularity surely goes a long way in the efforts to preserve them. It also appears to reflect a certain reverence for tradition and symbol that many still hold dear in an increasingly modernized world. In his introduction to *Lighthouses of the Maine Coast and the Men Who Keep Them*, Robert Coffin elegantly defines the poetry of the lighthouse: "Our lighthouses are more than mere guides to mariners . . . more than mere havens of peace. They are close to the things that count most with a poet. Close to the patterns of the tide and the passing of hours, sunrise, sunset, night. Close to solitude from which the best music comes. Close to storms and birds on the wing—patterns of a life that does not change, designs in the everlasting things." In humanity's quest for a symbol of steadfastness with universal appeal, a glimmer of permanence in an ephemeral age, evidence that something made by humankind can withstand the tests of nature and of time, the lighthouse stands as the perfect symbol.

OPPOSITE
With its distinctive black-and-white swirl, Cape Hatteras Lighthouse is one of the most widely recognized towers and serves as the state symbol of North Carolina.
Buxton, North Carolina

Lighthouse Collectibles

Not only do fans of lighthouses make it a point to visit as many lighthouses as possible on their travels around the country, but they buy anything and everything related to their favorite subject. Appearing on everything from T-shirts to blankets, housewares to coffee mugs, nightlights to Christmas ornaments, lighthouses manifest themselves over all manner of collectible items. Lighthouse buffs are so numerous that one business thrives entirely on this theme. The Lighthouse Depot in Wells, Maine—self-billed as "the world's largest lighthouse gift and collectible store"—devotes itself exclusively to merchandise featuring lighthouses.